Get To Grips With The Helping Hands

Latch on to life skills with the hands-on approach to the demands and challenges of everyday life

By

Rhona Birrell Weisen

Published by

MELROSE BOOKS

An Imprint of Melrose Press Limited
St Thomas Place, Ely
Cambridgeshire
CB7 4GG, UK
www.melrosebooks.com

FIRST EDITION

Cover and illustrations designed by *Maddie*

ISBN 1 905226 44 6

Printed and bound in Great Britain by:
CPI Antony Rowe, Bumpers Farm,
Chippenham, Wiltshire, SN14 6LH, UK

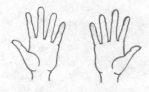

For Mathias and Thierry, with love

Thank you to family and friends who read
the draft of this book for their
encouragement and support.

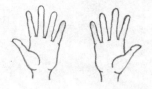

Acknowledgement

The life skills described in this book are based on a list and definition first published by the World Health Organization (Geneva) in the document *Life Skills Education in Schools* (WHO, 1993).

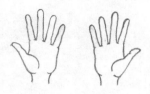

Preface

Helping Hands is an introduction to 10 must-have life skills. It's an easy way to learn more about yourself, how you interact with others and how you deal with day-to-day situations. All you need to learn about the Helping Hands is some free time and some 'life time' – that's the time you allow yourself to think about very human things, like how to be a happy and responsible person.

The Helping Hands will be more meaningful to you if you make notes when what you read triggers thoughts or questions about your own experiences. When you want to remember the life skills described in this book, try drawing the pictures that are used, they are easy to copy. Adapt the pictures to suit your needs ... whatever it takes to make the Helping Hands yours.

This book is addressed to you, but by all means involve other people by discussing what you read with the people who support you most.

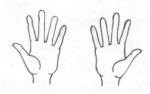

Contents

Who Needs A Helping Hand?   11

10 Fingers = 10 Skills   15

Creative and Critical Thinking – It's OK   21

Communication and Caring – Make Your Point   29

Decision Making and Problem Solving –
  Get on Top of Things   37

Expressing Emotions and Reducing Stress –
  Keep Connected   47

Self-Awareness and Empathy – The Underlying 'I'   55

Picture the Helping Hands   65

Strengthen the Helping Hands   71

Situations Where You Could Use a Helping Hand   73

Life Skills At Your Fingertips!   85

Practice Makes … Prepared   89

The Helping Hands Poem   93

Put Your Hands Together For A Better Life   97

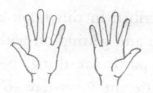

Who Needs A Helping Hand?

Who needs a helping hand? Don't we all!

With a bit of luck you are getting support from people who care for you. Life is beautiful and let's hope you're having fun. But life can be difficult too, and you may feel sad or worried at times. You can't always depend on other people to help you. You need to think about what it means to be responsible for yourself.

This book describes a special pair of Helping Hands. They are imaginary, but they can be as useful as the real ones when it comes to shaping your life. Since they are imaginary, you can have Helping Hands even if for some reason you've not got all your fingers available.

Following the advice in this book, you can learn how the hands serve as a reminder of 10 life skills. Life skills are abilities that help you to deal with the demands and challenges of everyday life. As a way to get to grips with demands and challenges, the Helping Hands can be part of your preparation for contributing to and adapting to the world around you. The Helping Hands give you a feel of what it takes to be fair and kind, open and understanding, happy and independent.

The life skills described in this book are about making the most of being human and getting on with living. They are not skills for doing any particular thing, because you can apply them in so many different ways day to day and throughout your life. You don't need to wait until you're in trouble to seek a Helping Hand.

Life is full of demands. Do this, do that! You need to be able to react to so many different situations.

* *Have you ever felt under pressure to do something that you didn't really want to do?*
* *Have you ever been unable to say what you wanted to for fear of being teased?*
* *Have you ever been in a situation where you didn't know what to do for the best?*

Sometimes, there are many different demands on you at once and life can seem overwhelming.

Life is full of challenges. It's up to you to show what your strengths are. You need to be able to act, not just react, to show what you are capable of doing.

* *Have you ever avoided a situation because you felt unable to manage?*
* *Have you ever let others do things for you that you could easily do yourself?*
* *Have you ever been surprised to find that you can do something that other people thought you couldn't do?*

You need to recognise the opportunities that are open to you and accept the effort that is needed to find your way in life.

Using this book, you can learn how to keep basic notions about 10 essential life skills close at hand. You never know when you will be confronted with the next demand or challenge, so prepare yourself by learning life skills in a way that is easily applied in day-to-day situations. The Helping Hands remind you of life skills that you can use to help yourself.

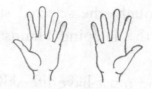

10 Fingers = 10 Skills

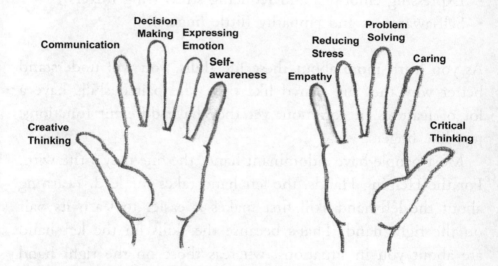

The Helping Hands

Here they are! On the Helping Hands, each finger is associated with a life skill. There are many, many skills that you will learn throughout your life; this book focuses on a set of 10 essential skills that lie at the heart of dealing with the demands and challenges of life.

As you read about the Helping Hands, you'll discover how they can remind you about important aspects of each of these life skills. Luckily enough, the selected skills are a convenient number for creating the Helping Hands: there are 10 fingers and 10 skills.

Just like fingers, the must-have life skills can be grouped as five pairs, as follows:

- Creative thinking and critical thinking (thumbs);
- Communication and caring (index fingers);
- Decision making and problem solving (middle fingers);
- Expressing emotions and reducing stress (ring fingers);
- Self-awareness and empathy (little fingers).

As you learn more about these life skills, you will understand better why they are paired like this. The paired skills have a lot of features in common, yet they have different functions, just like fingers.

Most people have a dominant hand, the one they write with. For the Helping Hands, the left hand takes the lead. Learning about the left-hand skill first makes it easier to learn its pair on the right hand. That's because the skills on the left hand are about you in situations, whereas those on the right hand are a bit more complicated; they are about you and others in situations.

Hold up your hands, palms facing you. Wiggle the appropriate finger as you say each skill out loud, to make the connection between a finger and a skill. If necessary, imagine a pair of Helping Hands and do this exercise mentally – in your thoughts.

The thumb

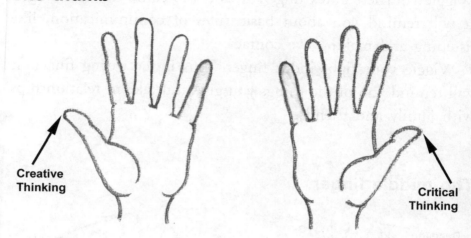

Creative
Thinking

Critical
Thinking

Wiggle your left thumb. This is the creative-thinking thumb. It will remind you to go beyond the barriers that limit your thinking, to come up with new ideas.

Wiggle your right thumb. This is the critical-thinking thumb. It will remind you to see things as they are, to see strengths and limits at the same time.

The index finger

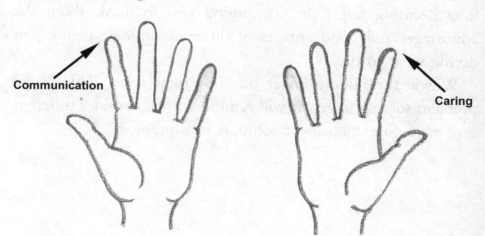

Communication

Caring

Wiggle your left index finger. This is the communicator finger. It will remind you about basic rules of communication, like listening and making eye contact.

Wiggle your right index finger. This is the caring finger. It will remind you of the things you give and take in relationships with family and friends.

The middle finger

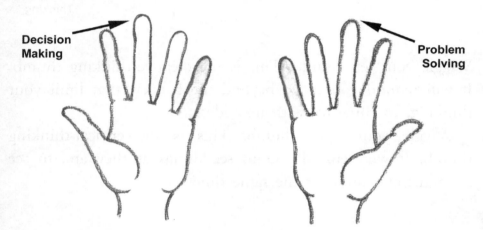

Wiggle the middle finger on your left hand. This is the long deciding finger. It will remind you to think about the advantages and disadvantages of different options, before you decide what to do.

Wiggle the middle finger on your right hand. This is the problem-solving finger. It will remind you to consider different actions, before choosing a solution to a problem.

The ring finger

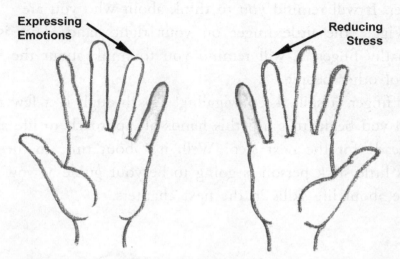

Wiggle the ring finger on your left hand. This is the emotional finger. It will remind you to accept your emotions and to express them in an appropriate way.

Wiggle the ring finger on your right hand. This is the stress-detector finger. It will remind you to recognise stress and reduce the tension that it creates.

The little finger

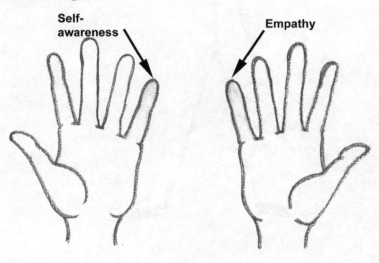

Wiggle the little finger on your left hand. This is the little 'I' finger. It will remind you to think about who you are.

Wiggle the little finger on your right hand. This is the empathy finger. It will remind you to think about the inner self of other people.

A finger, a skill, keep wiggling! Go through it a few times until you begin to grasp this hands-on approach to life skills.

Ready for the next step? Well, it's about time to meet **U**. This little stick person is going to be your guide as you learn more about life skills in the next chapters.

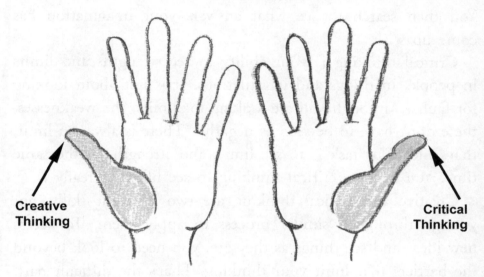

Creative and Critical Thinking – It's Ok

Creative Thinking

Critical Thinking

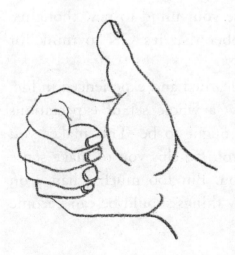

The thumbs on the Helping Hands remind you of creative thinking and critical thinking. Did you know that when you put your thumbs up it means OK? Well, put your thumbs up because it's OK to think your own creative thoughts and it's OK to use critical thinking. In fact, it is really important that you learn to do so.

Creative thinking is your ability to come up with new ideas. When you are looking for a new idea, you need to be able to draw on your knowledge and experiences, to find the relevant information to put into new thoughts. It's a bit like doing maths; you take a fraction of one experience, add a fraction of another experience, then multiply by some knowledge. But don't worry, your imagination does this calculation for you! Your job is to fill your mind with relevant images and thoughts. You then search to see what answers your imagination has come up with.

Critical thinking is your ability to see strengths and limits in people, in things and in situations. It is not about looking for faults. Although you are looking for limits, the weaknesses, these don't have to be seen as negative. There is always a limit, that's life! Your task is to see limits and strengths at the same time. You can use critical thinking to see life as it really is.

Creative and critical thinking are two different skills, but you go through a similar process to apply them. To access new ideas and see things as they are, you need to look beyond the barriers that limit your thinking. That's the difficult part, recognising the barriers that close your mind to new thoughts. Well, the first step is to remember that it's OK to think for yourself.

Depending on what you have learned and experienced in life, you will have developed by now a whole set of expectations and opinions about how things ought to be. This makes you feel more confident and in control. It helps you to make sense of life and the world around you. But too much reliance on expectations and opinions of how things should be can become a barrier to thinking.

Creative and critical thoughts that are useful to you don't always match your expectations, and they don't always match what others expect from you. Biased opinions get in the way of creative and critical thinking because they close your mind to many valuable thoughts and ideas. They are social barriers to open-minded thinking.

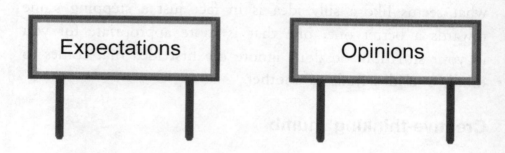

Another type of barrier to thinking is caused by your emotions. Your doubts and fears depend on what you have learned and experienced. Doubts and fears protect you from thinking and doing things that could be distressing. These emotional barriers to thinking typically pop up in new situations, when you feel vulnerable. However, it will encourage you to know that behind emotional barriers lie a whole bundle of thoughts that could actually be quite good for you ... if you dare to look!

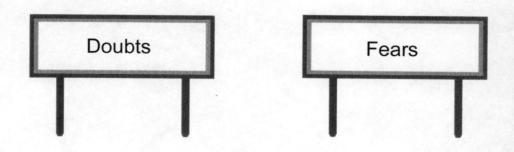

Getting over the barriers to creative and critical thinking is something that you do mentally, in your thoughts. That way, it is not such a threatening thing to do. Social and emotional barriers don't go away so easily, but at times you will need to make an effort to go beyond them.

If you find that you think strange, uncomfortable thoughts you don't need to act on them, just notice them. Sometimes what seems like a silly idea is in fact just a stepping stone towards a better one, one that is more appropriate for you in your situation. So don't ignore the first idea that comes to mind, one idea leads to another.

Creative-thinking thumb

Prepare yourself for creative thinking. This will be especially useful when you are in a situation where you have no idea what to do for the best. You're stuck, you don't know what to do...

Picture 1 shows **U**, our stick friend, with two bags, one contains knowledge; the other, experiences. To find new ideas, **U** has to hold on to these two bags and jump over the social and emotional barriers that limit creativity.

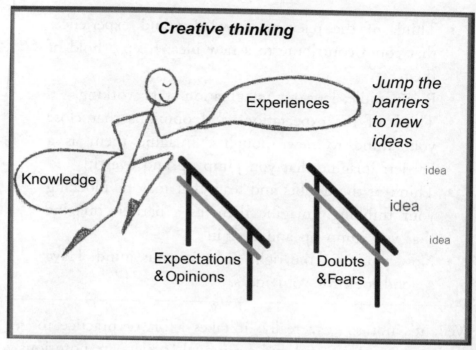

Creative thinking

Experiences

Jump the
barriers
to new
ideas

Knowledge

Expectations
& Opinions

Doubts
& Fears

idea

idea

idea

Picture 1

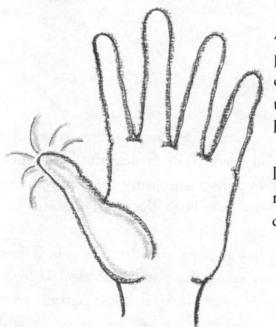

As you look at this picture and think about creative thinking, wiggle the thumb on your left hand.

The next time you are looking for a new idea, remember this picture of creative thinking.

- Think of the relevant knowledge and experiences that could contribute to a new idea. Keep a hold of them.
- Relax, smile, let your imagination start working.
- Think of the expectations and opinions that close your mind to new thoughts. Imagine them as a barrier: imagine that you jump up and over it!
- Think of the doubts and fears that may be blocking your thinking. Imagine them as a barrier: imagine that you jump up and over it!
- Now, you're in the right place in your mind. Have a good look for your ideas.

Well, it's not so easy really; it takes a bit of practice to get the balance right. Social and emotional barriers are notoriously difficult to clear. But why not put a smile on your face, like **U,** and give it a go.

Critical-thinking thumb

Learning to jump the barriers to creative thinking paves the way for critical thinking. You need to use critical thinking when you can only see one side of something: only the strengths or only the limits. Your task is to see both the strengths and the limits at the same time.

Picture 2 shows **U** looking at a picture on the wall. There are social and emotional barriers in the way which stop **U** from seeing the picture properly. **U** needs to push these barriers over to think critically about the picture, to see its strengths and

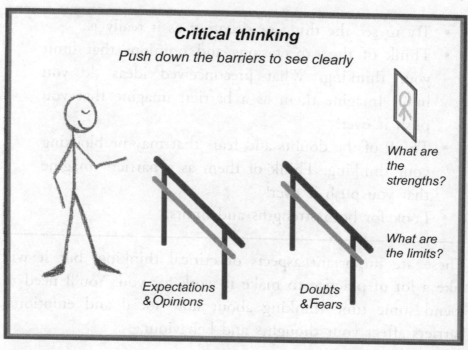

Critical thinking

Push down the barriers to see clearly

What are the strengths?

What are the limits?

Expectations & Opinions

Doubts & Fears

Picture 2

limits. As you look at this picture and think about critical thinking, wiggle the thumb on your right hand.

The next time you need to be more open-minded, remember this picture of critical thinking.

- Try to see the thing or situation as it really is.
- Think of the expectations and opinions that limit your thinking. What preconceived ideas do you have? Imagine them as a barrier: imagine that you push it over!
- Think of the doubts and fears that may be blocking your thinking. Think of them as a barrier: imagine that you push it over!
- Look for both strengths and limits.

These are important aspects of critical thinking, but it will take a lot of practice to make it work for you. You'll need to spend some time thinking about how social and emotional barriers affect your thoughts and behaviour.

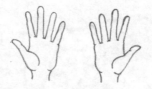

Communication and Caring
– Make Your Point

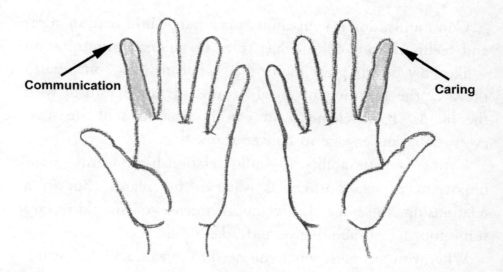

Communication   **Caring**

The index fingers on the Helping Hands remind you of communication and caring. The index finger is especially good for pointing the way ahead. Use it to remind you of how important it is to make your point – express yourself in conversation and in relationships with family and friends.

Communication is your ability to exchange information, ideas and feelings. Your culture has rules to guide communication – like how people greet each other, when to look someone in the eye, the meaning of facial expressions and gestures with the hands. Basic elements of communication skill are used every time you engage in conversation.

Caring is your ability to build relationships. Caring is as important in relationships as water is for plants. But in a relationship, you not only give nourishment, you should receive some too. It's all about give and take.

When you recognise what you need to put into a relationship to make it grow, you will be able to see what others should be giving you. In healthy relationships you go through life with the support you need to deal with the difficult times, and the company you need to make the most of the good times.

Communication and caring are two different skills, but they both help you to assess the quality of your interactions with others. As skills, communication and caring are reduced to their key elements; you can become more aware of what is expected from you, and what you can expect from others.

The rules of social interaction are complicated. Some aspects are explained to you; the rest seem to be unspoken rules that you learn by observing other people. They provide structure and flow to your interactions, like in a ball game.

Not following the rules of communication and caring will cause you problems. It causes confusion – people won't know how to relate to you. For instance, if you nod your head (as if to say yes) but you say no, who knows what you really want to say! If you are always on the receiving end in relationships, always accepting support, but not prepared to give any, then you may lose friends.

Unfortunately, people are quick to make judgements about others based on things like clothes and accent. Have you ever noticed how your appearance and behaviour affect the way that other people interact with you? If your T-shirt is back to front, or you've had the same one on for a week, this will create difficulties in interacting on equal terms with others.

Judging people as 'like me' or 'not like me' is another way to organise the interaction between people. However, on the whole, we are not good at judging people like this, and most often it disrupts rather than improves the flow in the exchange between people.

Being aware of the rules that guide communication and caring will help you to be more understanding when you meet people from other cultures, who don't use the same rules as you do. Learn to notice when other people are using rules that are different from your own.

Communicator finger

Prepare yourself for communication by thinking about what happens in a short conversation. Basic rules of communication are involved each time you do this. It can be difficult to use communication skills. At times, you may feel shy, especially in a situation that is new to you. Sometimes, you may find it difficult to say what you want to say, for fear of being humiliated or rejected.

Picture 3 shows **U** playing tennis. This is a special game of conversational tennis. When you converse with someone, you need to think about the back-and-forth flow in conversation.

In tennis, no player should keep the ball all the time. It's the same in conversation: no one should speak all the time; and, if

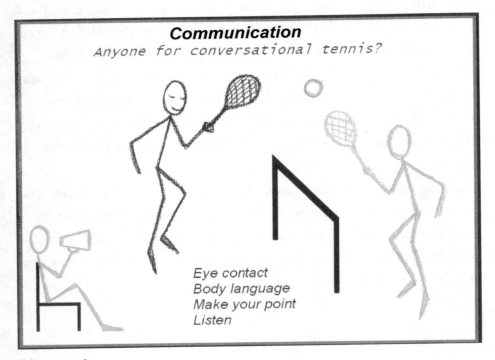

Picture 3

there is no reply, it's like when the other player doesn't return the ball, this interrupts the flow of conversational tennis. In Picture 3, **U** is being helped by a coach, who shouts out some basic rules.

As you look at this picture and think about communication, wiggle the index finger on your left hand.

The next time you have difficulty expressing your opinion, think about this picture of communication, remember what the coach says to **U**.

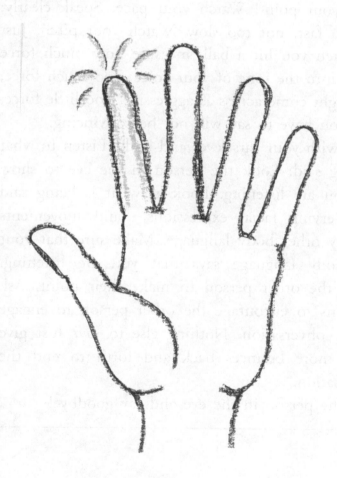

- Look the person in the eye and say hi!
- Talk with your mouth, your eyes and your body. Make eye contact to show that you want the other person to listen to you. When speaking, you should make eye contact as much as possible, at least at the beginning and end of each sentence. Be aware of your body language. Does your body agree with what you are saying?
- Make your point! Watch your pace. Speak clearly: not too fast, not too slow. Watch your pitch. Just like when you hit a ball, measure how much force to put into the tone of your voice. Too much force, you might come across as aggressive. Too little force, what you have to say will not be convincing.
- Listen with your ears, eyes and body. Listen to what is being said. Look the person in the eye to show that you are listening. Look at what is being said by observing facial expressions, hand movements and any other body language. Make sure that your own body language says that you are listening.
  • Help the other person to make their point. Ask questions to encourage the other person to engage in the conversation. Nothing else to say? Just give a few more bounces back and forth to end the conversation.
- Look the person in the eye and say goodbye!

Caring finger

Practising effective communication prepares you for another life skill, caring. Prepare yourself for the next time you need to exercise your caring skills. You'll need to think carefully about caring if you find that you are having difficulty relating to the people closest to you, your family and friends. Perhaps someone needs your help or it could be you who needs support.

Picture 4 shows **U** having a game of basketball. OK, it could be football if you prefer. Imagine that **U** is passing the ball back and forth to other team members. You can think about relationships in this way, it's all about give and take, passing the ball back and forth as you run towards your goal.

Reaching your goals in life can be difficult and you'll need

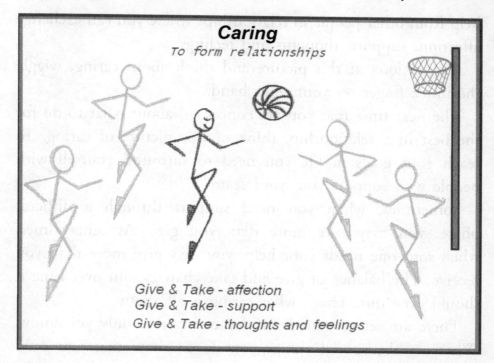

Caring
To form relationships

Give & Take - affection
Give & Take - support
Give & Take - thoughts and feelings

Picture 4

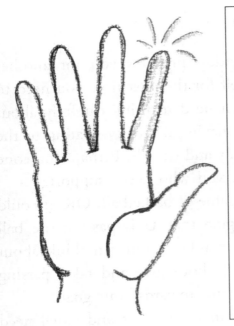

- Give affection (be kind, give compliments) &
- Take affection (accept kindness, accept compliments).
- Give support (listen, offer help) &
- Take support (ask for help, accept help).
- Give (share) your thoughts and feelings &
- Take (share) other people's thoughts and feelings.

help from other people in relationships where you can exchange affection, support, thoughts and feelings.

As you look at this picture and think about caring, wiggle the index finger on your right hand.

The next time that you are concerned about what to do for the best in a relationship, think of this picture of caring. To reach your goals in life you need to surround yourself with people who support you, your team.

Sometimes, when you need support through a difficult phase, you may take more than you give. At other times, when someone needs your help, you may give more than you receive. The balance of give and take changes, but over time it should even out. That's what caring is all about.

There are secret ingredients for caring that only you know. What are the special things you do to show that you care? Can you think of some?

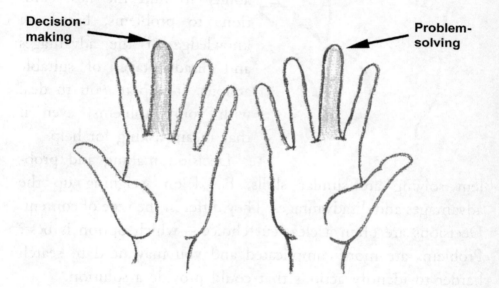

Decision Making and Problem Solving – Get on Top of Things

Decision-making

Problem-solving

The middle fingers on the Helping Hands remind you of decision making and problem solving. They lie on the longest fingers of your hands to encourage you to keep on top of things. Don't let life get out of control: make decisions and solve problems as they come along. That's how you keep ahead and moving on.

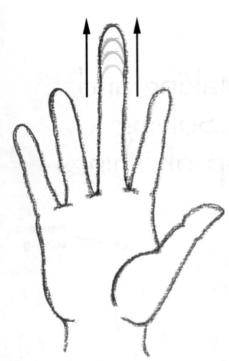

Decision making is your ability to make informed choices, based on knowledge of the advantages and disadvantages of the options available to you. Your aim is to make positive decisions, which bring the most advantages.

Problem solving is your ability to find the best solutions to problems, based on knowledge of the advantages and disadvantages of suitable actions. It's up to you to deal with your problems, even if that means asking for help.

Decision making and problem solving are similar skills, based on weighing up the advantages and disadvantages. They differ in the type of content. Decisions are often a clear-cut choice – which option is best? Problems are more complicated and you may need to search harder to identify actions that could provide a solution.

By making decisions and solving problems you can actively contribute to creating a good life for yourself. You don't need to wait for an important decision or big problem before you start thinking about decision-making and problem-solving skills. You can start by becoming aware of all the ways in which you make decisions and solve problems day to day.

You may feel at times that you don't really choose for yourself, but you do, at least to some extent. If you look closely at your life, there are lots of decisions that you make and problems that you solve. Notice how your choices affect the outcomes of everyday situations. Notice how you are responsible for your actions.

Sometimes you may want to let others deal with decisions and problems for you. That's understandable, it can be scary when you don't know if you're making the right choice. That's why it's good to develop a strategy for making decisions and solving problems. Going through decision making and problem solving step by step allows you to break a big decision, or a big problem, into smaller parts that are easier to think about.

If you feel overwhelmed by a situation and you feel you can't manage on your own, ask a trusted friend or family member to sit down with you, to go through the steps together. Gradually you will become more confident in your ability to make choices.

Sometimes you may be disappointed; the choice you make might not always give the result you want. That happens. Life doesn't always go the way we plan. When your choice is not having the effect you had hoped for, think again.

Making decisions and solving problems can mean bringing about changes in your life. Changes are a bit of a challenge, but don't forget that positive changes bring progress. That's what decision making and problem solving should be about – the most positive choices for making progress in your life.

Long deciding finger

Prepare yourself for decision making. When it is difficult to decide what to do, you may feel tempted to choose what

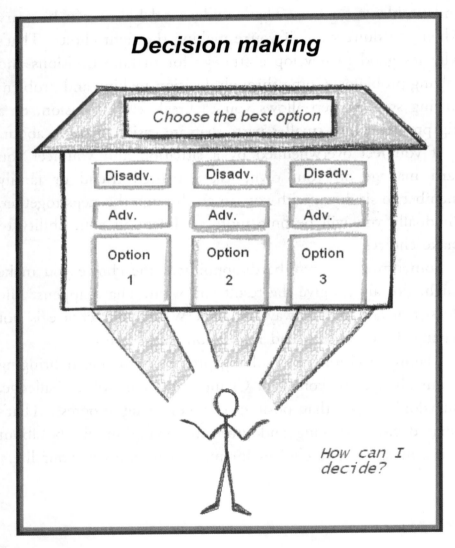

Picture 5

seems to please other people. Or, perhaps you want to put off deciding until tomorrow... Well, it's about time to learn about decision making as a skill.

Picture 5 shows **U** in front of a house that is split into three parts. Each part has a door, which is a different option. Imagine **U** opens the door and goes inside to explore the first part of the house, option 1. On the first floor, **U** looks around and notes all the advantages. On the second floor, **U** notes all the disadvantages.

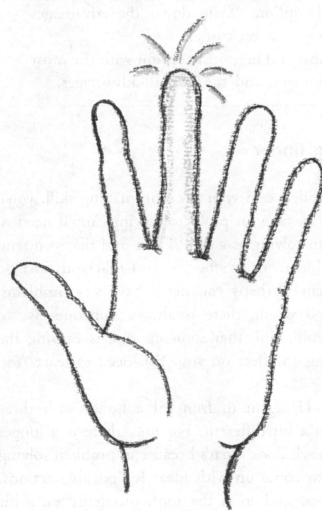

U goes through the other doors, to explore the rest of the house in the same way. Then **U** goes up to the attic to decide which is the best option.

As you look at this picture and think about decision making, wiggle the middle finger on your left hand.

The next time that you have a difficult choice to make, think about the decision-making house.

> - What decision has to be made? Write it down.
> - Identify three options – think of three different things that you could decide to do. Write them down and if need be discuss your options with someone you trust.
> - Consider each option. Write down the advantages and disadvantages of each one.
> - Choose the most and best – the option with the most and best advantages, and the least disadvantages.

Problem-solving finger

Once you gain confidence in your decision-making skill, you'll feel more prepared to take on problem solving. You'll need to think about problem solving as a skill if you find that you tend to ignore your problems, or maybe you feel that you can't do anything about them. Perhaps you never have any problems, because if things go wrong there is always someone else to blame…! Even if you think that someone else is causing the problem, it is having an effect on you. You need to react. You need to act.

Picture 6 shows **U**, again in front of a house with three parts. This house is a bit different. For one, there is a longer path leading up to each door. That's because in problem solving it can take longer to come up with ideas for possible actions. The doors are arched and so is the roof; problems are a bit less clear-cut than decisions. Often, decisions are just about you. More often, problems are about you and situations you get into with other people.

To come up with a solution, **U** opens each door and goes inside to explore the advantages and disadvantages of each

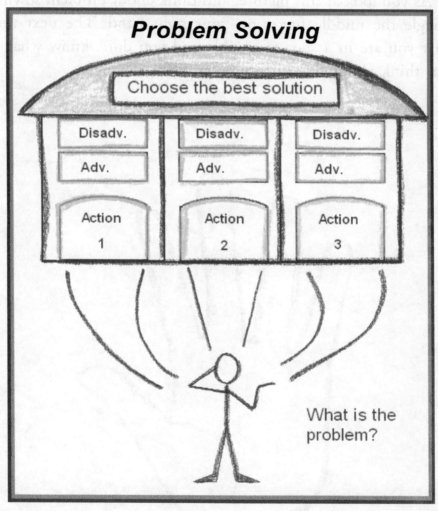

Picture 6

action. **U** needs to explore all three parts of the house, before going to the attic to consider which action has the most and the best advantages, and the least disadvantages. **U** can then choose the best action and apply this to help solve the problem.

As you look at this picture, and think about problem solving, wiggle the middle finger on your right hand. The next time that you are in a spot of trouble and you don't know what to do, think about this picture of problem solving.

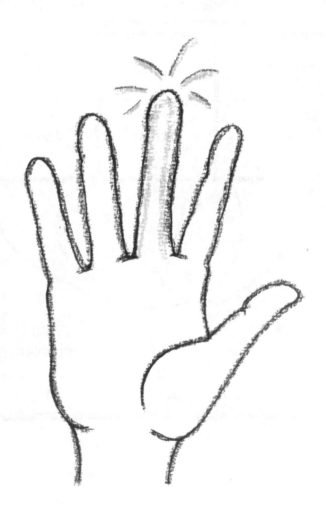

- What is the problem? Write it down. What are the facts: what has happened; what/who is causing it; and how does it make you feel? How did you react and what effect did that have?
- Identify three possible actions that you could take to help solve the problem. Write them down, and if need be seek advice from someone you trust.
- Consider each action. Write down the advantages and disadvantages of each one.
- Choose the most and best – the solution with the most and best advantages, and the least disadvantages.

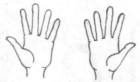

Expressing Emotions and Reducing Stress – Keep Connected

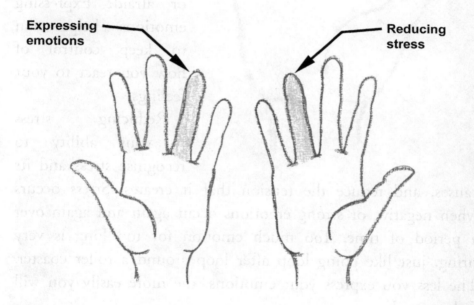

Expressing emotions

Reducing stress

The ring fingers on the Helping Hands remind you of expressing emotions and reducing stress. The ring finger of the left hand is traditionally for wedding rings, to show the connection between married couples. Use the ring fingers to remind you to keep connected with your emotions and how you react to stress.

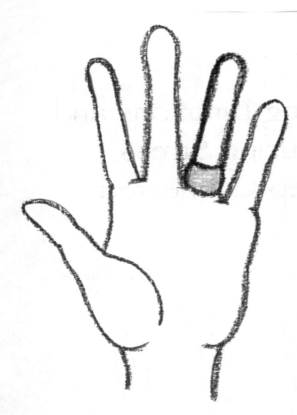

Expressing emotions is your ability to recognise and accept your emotions, and show your emotions in an appropriate way. Emotions are all those strong feelings you have, like when you feel happy or sad, angry or afraid. Expressing emotions helps you to keep control of how you react to your feelings.

Reducing stress is your ability to recognise stress and its causes, and reduce the tension that it creates. Stress occurs when negative or strong emotions occur again and again over a period of time. Too much emotion for too long is very tiring, just like going loop after loop around a roller coaster. The less you express your emotions, the more easily you will feel stressed.

Expressing emotions and reducing stress are two different life skills, but they are both about being able to perceive and manage emotions. They are both about coping, with short bursts of emotion (expressing emotions), or with longer- lasting emotional states (reducing stress).

Emotions are normal and and can be very useful. When

you feel nervous before an exam, the improved concentration that this creates may help you to perform well. When you feel fear, you become more alert, which helps if you need to protect yourself. Emotions bring about changes in your mind and body that prepare you to deal with demanding situations. That's why it is so important to recognise and accept your emotions.

If you let an emotion get out of control, it no longer serves its purpose. Sometimes emotions can be overwhelming and you may not know how to express what you feel. You may become overemotional at times.

- *Have you ever reacted more strongly than you really meant to?*
- *Have you ever shouted angrily at someone when what you really wanted to say was a polite 'no thanks'!*

Keep connected, do your thoughts and feelings really match the situation?

One way to stop emotions from heating up and boiling over is to express emotions when you feel them. Perhaps you could tell someone what is bothering you. It will help others to understand you better and they may be able to provide support. Keep connected and under control to turn difficult situations into challenges, not catastrophes!

At times, you may try to hide your emotions because you feel embarrassed to show how sad or afraid you really are. Sometimes your mind tries to hide your feelings from you. That's how you protect yourself from unpleasant feelings. But all emotions need to be expressed in some way, once felt inside they need a way out of your body.

You need to find positive ways to release emotions. That's why it can be good to find an activity that helps you to relax or let off steam. What things make you feel better – sport, hobbies, a good joke…? Humour can be a good way to release emotions, that's why people sometimes say: 'If I didn't laugh, I'd cry'.

Emotional finger

Prepare yourself for expressing emotions. This will be especially important if you tend to allow your emotions to take over, in an uncontrolled way, or if you tend to hide emotions, hoping they'll just go away.

Picture 7 shows **U** on an emotional roller coaster. You get on

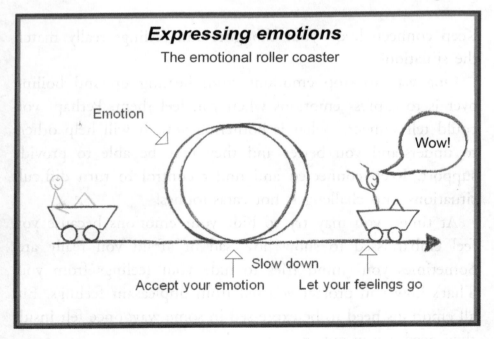

Picture 7

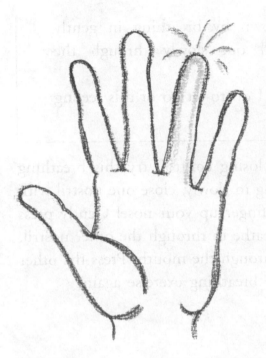

an emotional roller coaster like this every time an experience triggers a strong emotion. Whoosh ... off you go into the emotional loop, all upside down and out of control. When this happens, feel the emotion, accept it, but don't let it last too long. The only way off this roller coaster is to calm down and express the emotion you feel. As you look at this image and think about expressing emotions, wiggle the ring finger on your left hand.

The next time you feel that you are losing control, remember this picture of expressing emotions.

Notice when you are just about to go through an emotional roller coaster loop.

- What kind of thoughts do you have? What are the sensations in your body? How are you behaving?
- Think about the situation that caused you to feel this emotion. Does your emotion really match the situation?
- Accept your emotion, even if it's inappropriate, you are feeling it.
- Decide to take control of your emotion.

- Slow down – calm down by breathing in gently through the nose and out slowly through the mouth.
- Ask yourself: What can I do to let go of this feeling in a suitable way?

When you feel that you are losing control, try this breathing exercise. To focus on breathing in slowly, close one nostril with a finger – no, don't put the finger up your nose! Gently press one side of your nose and breathe in through the other nostril. Release. Breathe out slowly through the mouth. Press the other side of your nose and do the breathing exercise again.

Stress-detector finger

Learning to cope with emotions should help to prevent you from becoming too stressed. But sometimes stress builds up gradually before you notice, so prepare yourself for reducing stress. You'll need to learn to relax if you find that you are suffering from symptoms of stress, such as headaches, poor concentration and trouble getting to sleep at night.

Picture 8 shows our friend **U** on a very stressful roller coaster. Loop after loop, **U** experiences unpleasant emotions. Wouldn't that be exhausting? Even too much fun can be stressful, if you are constantly active and never relax. To get off the stressful roller coaster, **U** needs to recognise the stress caused by too much emotion. U needs to slow down and think positively to regain control.

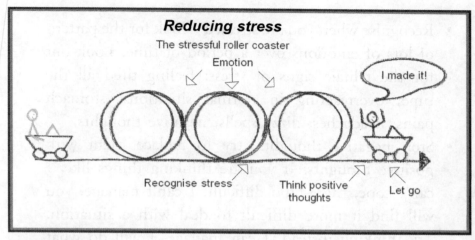

Picture 8

As you look at this picture and think about coping with stress, wiggle the ring finger on your right hand. The next time that you begin to feel overwhelmed, tense, tearful ..., remember this picture of reducing stress.

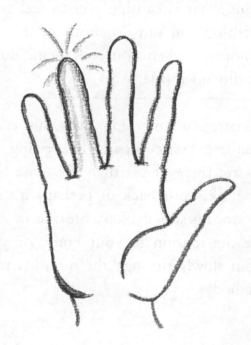

- Recognise when you are stressed – look for the pattern of lots of emotions over a period of time. Look out for the telltale signs of stress: feeling tired all the time; overreacting in normal situations; stomach pains; headaches; dizzy spells; negative thoughts.
- Stop negative thoughts, try to replace them with positive thoughts. If you are thinking things like, I can't cope, this is too difficult, I can't manage, you will find it more difficult to deal with a situation. Try thinking instead, I can manage, I will do what I can.
- Let go of the tension in your body. When you are stressed, your body becomes tense. Relax by giving yourself a good shake, then let your body go a bit softer all over.
- Think about what is causing you to feel stressed. Is there something you can do about it...?
- Express emotions when you feel them, don't allow them to build up inside.

When you feel stressed and tense, try this exercise. Clench one hand to make a fist, compare this feeling to other parts of your body – are there places that feel tense like your fist – your face, your neck, your back or perhaps it's your stomach? Where are you storing stress? Now, breathe in slowly through the nose, locate the tension in your body. As you open your hand, breathe out slowly through the mouth and let go of the tension in your body.

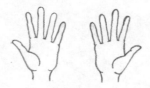

Self-Awareness and Empathy – The Underlying 'I'

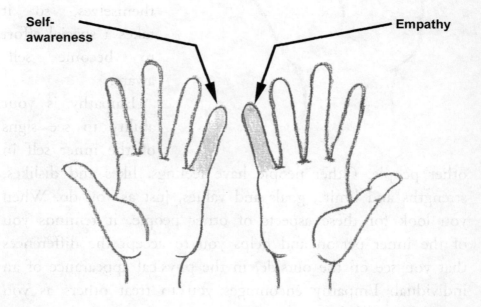

Self-awareness

Empathy

Last, but not least, the little fingers on the Helping Hands remind you of self-awareness and empathy. This is your reminder of I in me and in others. In some versions of sign language that is what the little finger means, I. The little fingers should remind you of the importance of knowing yourself and understanding other people better.

Self-awareness is your ability to know your inner self. It

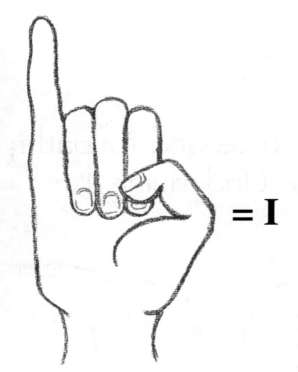

= I

involves keeping in touch with your feelings, likes and dislikes, strengths and limits, goals and values. People are good at hiding their real thoughts and feelings, especially thoughts about themselves, so it takes a special effort to become self-aware.

Empathy is your ability to see signs of the inner self in other people. Other people have feelings, likes and dislikes, strengths and limits, goals and values, just as you do. When you look for these aspects of other people, it reminds you of the inner person and helps you to accept the differences that you see on the outside, in the physical appearance of an individual. Empathy encourages you to treat others as you would like to be treated.

Self-awareness and empathy are different skills, but they are similar. They both provide information about the inner self. Becoming more aware and more accepting of yourself will make you a stronger person, and it will prepare you for being more aware and accepting of other people.

Being in touch with your own feelings will help you perceive feelings in others. When you observe what someone does and says, to get an idea about them, your understanding of the person depends on what it feels like to you when you do and say those things. The memory of your own experiences helps you to imagine what another person is thinking and feeling in similar situations.

When you observe an emotion in someone, even if that person is older, younger, fatter, thinner, darker or fairer, think about what that emotion feels like for you. What kind of things would you like people to say and do when you feel that emotion? That's how empathy can guide your interactions with others.

Empathy has to be kept active in your mind, so that it shows in your actions. Unfortunately, we humans do many things that show it is possible to forget that other people have feelings. Too often, we neglect the fact that other people have their own likes and dislikes, goals and values.

It is possible to go through life without being self-aware. Often, it is only when there is a crisis that people stop to take a proper look at themselves. Likewise, it is possible to interact with others without stopping to consider who the other person is. In this case, interaction with other people becomes superficial.

Self-awareness requires that you look at yourself without judgement. You need to accept yourself as you are. Empathy is the same, look at others without judgement and accept them as they are. These two life skills are so difficult to put into practice because we judge others and ourselves too much. This seems to be a way to avoid looking below the surface, as if to make life easier. Let's face it, life is not so simple.

You have to keep being self-aware because you are changing. Each time you experience a big event, you change a little bit. That's why it's easy to lose touch with your real self. The people around you are changing too. Realising the changes in yourself will help you to appreciate and accept changes in other people.

Self-awareness and empathy go hand in hand to keep you in touch with the inside. Use the little I fingers to scratch beneath the surface of life, this is where happiness is found.

Little I finger

Think about self-awareness. You'll notice that you lack self-awareness if an activity that used to please you no longer gives satisfaction, because it is not what you really want to do at all. Or, if you feel depressed, you might find that you can't think of anything positive about yourself. Look inside to remember the good in you.

Picture 9 shows **U** dressed up to show different aspects of self-awareness. To develop self-awareness you have to ask yourself questions about who you are and what you want out of life. Think your way through this very deep question by considering your likes and dislikes, your limits and strengths, your feelings, your goals and values. As you look at this image and think about self-awareness, wiggle the little finger on your left hand.

The next time that you don't feel confident and you have negative thoughts about yourself, remember this picture of self-awareness.

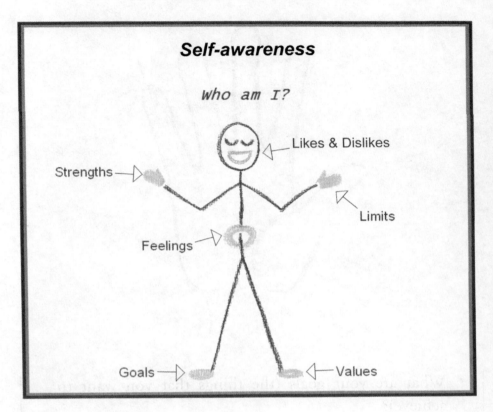

Picture 9

- Ask the big question, Who am I? Be as positive as you can be.
- What do you like or enjoy most in life? What are the things that you don't like?
- What are your strengths (what are you good at, what is good about you)?
- What are your limits (what are you not so good at, what are your weaknesses)?
- What are your feelings? Which emotion have you felt most often in the past week?

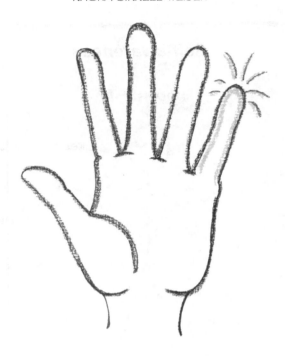

- What are your goals (the things that you want to achieve)?
- What are your values (the principles that are important to you – like justice, equality, happiness, etc.)?

If the image you have of yourself is not what you want it to be, it's important to ask yourself if it is reasonable to see yourself in those terms. Are you being too hard on yourself? You don't need to do that. We all have strengths. We all have limits.

When you find that there are aspects of yourself that you want to change, ask yourself: Why am I like this? Think about your limits; do you know anyone with similar difficulties? How do they overcome them? Could those ideas apply to you?

Empathy finger

All the work that you do to become more self-aware will help you as you prepare to feel and show more empathy. Empathy will be really useful if you tend to judge people by the way they look.

Picture 10 shows **U** inside another body! That is what empathy is like, all those questions that are important about you are important for other people too. This is how you can begin to see the I in others. To develop empathy, you have to ask yourself questions about the other person's likes and dislikes, strengths and limits, feelings, goals and values. To

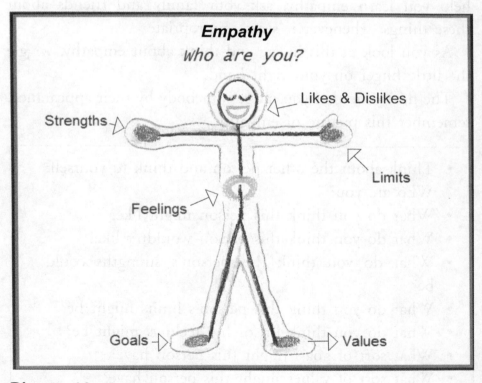

Picture 10

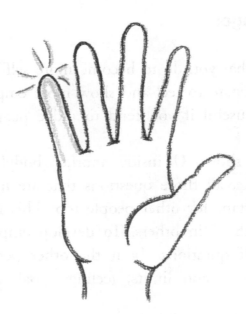

help you learn empathy, ask your family and friends about these things, whenever it seems appropriate.

As you look at this image and think about empathy, wiggle the little finger on your right hand.

The next time that you judge somebody by their appearance, remember this picture of empathy.

- Think about the other person and think to yourself: Who are you?
- What do you think this person might like?
- What do you think this person wouldn't like?
- What do you think this person's strengths could be?
- What do you think this person's limits might be?
- What do you think his or her feelings might be?
- What sort of goals might this person have?
- What sort of values might this person have?

Your aim is to ask these questions about other people. You are not expected to know all the answers. Often, for empathy, you can only guess. If you expect to know all the answers, you won't use empathy very often! Empathy is most important when you meet someone that you don't know, because that is when you are most likely to make superficial judgements.

If you can learn to think about people in this way, the things you do, the things you ask, the things you see, will all gradually help you to know more about others and you will begin to interact at that deeper level, beneath the surface.

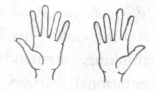

Picture the Helping Hands

Each finger on the Helping Hands reminds you of a life skill. Look at your hands, or think about the Helping Hands, which finger is which skill?

Remember the pictures of **U**? Well, if you want to have life skills on hand when you need them, it will help if you can recall those pictures when you think about each skill. They are a reminder of what you can do to apply the skills. To help you remember the pictures, they have been simplified to 10 symbols. This is the life skill code. Let's see if you can decode it.

What do you think this means?

Did you know that a light bulb symbol like this is used to suggest an idea? So this image shows a barrier to an idea... Can you think of the rest of the image? Do you remember **U** carrying two bags (of knowledge and experiences) and jumping over social and emotional barriers to find ideas? That's it! This is the symbol for creative thinking.

What do you think this means?
Ah ha, easy! This is, of course, critical thinking. Remember the social and emotional barriers that stop **U** from seeing the picture clearly?

What about this one?
It's **U** playing tennis, so this must be about communication. Remember all that bouncing back and forth of conversational tennis? The coach was encouraging **U** to listen, use appropriate body language, make eye contact and make a point.

And this one?

U playing ball again. Ah yes, wasn't it basketball? There's a lot of give and take required for caring, just like when you play ball in a team game. This is to remind you of what it takes to build relationships – give and take support, affection, thoughts and feelings.

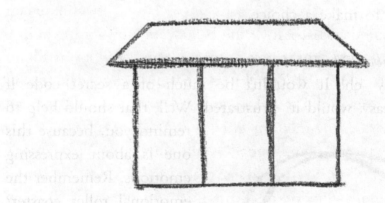

Here's an easy one.

Yes, the decision-making house. Remember, it has three parts, with three doors, one for each option. For each option, you consider advantages and disadvantages before going to the attic to make a choice. That's it!

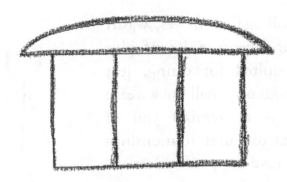

Another easy one.

Of course, it's the problem-solving house, with a rounded roof (because problems are less clear-cut than most decisions). Just like the decision-making house, there are three parts and each door is a possible action for solving the problem. For each action, you consider advantages and disadvantages before going to the attic to make a choice.

Now, how about this one?

A bit tricky, eh! It wouldn't be much of a secret code if it was too easy, would it? Frustrated? Well, that should help to remind you, because this one is about expressing emotions. Remember the emotional roller coaster? Learn to accept your emotions, but don't let them get out of control. After you've been through an emotional roller coaster, calm down by

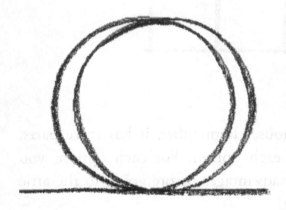

breathing in gently through the nose and out slowly through the mouth.

Even better, how about this one?
Yes, the very stressful roller coaster. Just think, your friends could get really stressed out trying to guess what that is. Remember, too much emotion, again and again, builds up to make you stressed. Recognise when you are stressed, think positive thoughts, find tension in your body and learn to let go.

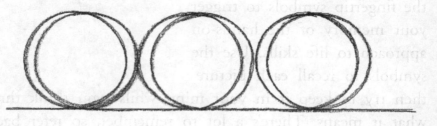

What about this one?
That's right, self-aware **U**, and all those questions about you – your likes and dislikes, strengths and limits, feelings, goals and values. All that to help you think about, Who am I?

And finally...

It's empathy, with **U** seeing what it's like to be someone else. All those questions about you can be asked about other people too. Try to see the I in other people.

The 10 symbols of the life skill code fit on the fingers of the Helping Hands. They are the fingertip symbols to trigger your memory of the hands-on approach to life skills. Use the symbols to recall each picture, then try to keep it in your mind whilst you think through what it means. There's a lot to remember, so refer back to previous chapters whenever you need to.

Picture the Helping Hands like this. No, it is not Chinese!

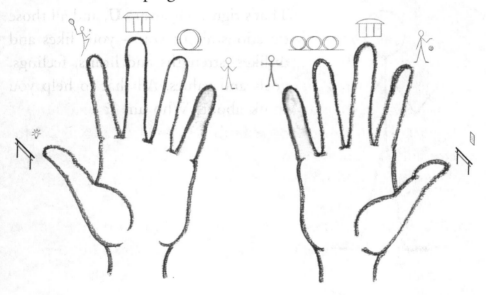

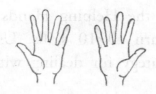

Strengthen the Helping Hands

So far, the Helping Hands have been described as 10 fingers and 10 skills. You have learned that the five skills on the left Helping Hand are closely related to the five skills on the right Helping Hand. It is easy to see that they have a lot in common. Put your hands together so that your fingers touch each other (or think about imaginary Helping Hands). As you push your fingers together, think about the five pairs of life skills. Notice how your fingers feel strong when you push them together. Life skills are like that: they are stronger if the paired skills support each other.

Sometimes you use life skills without even realising. That's just like hands. People do so many things with their hands without thinking about them. But there are also lots of tasks which require careful attention to how the hands are used. Similarly, in difficult or new situations you will need to concentrate on applying life skills.

Clasp your hands and notice how your fingers become linked. Even when you focus on one particular life skill, other skills will be used to support what you are trying to do. Used together, life skills, like fingers, work in a multitude of fine ways.

The life skills on the Helping Hands only become really strong when you learn all 10 skills. Use them together at the core of your strategy for dealing with the demands and challenges of life.

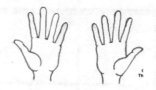

Situations Where You Could Use a Helping Hand

Let's face it, life can be complicated. Life is like a complex network of roads and paths, full of all sorts of obstacles and surprises. You go uphill, round sharp bends, on fast roads, bumpy roads, downhill, along narrow paths ... life has it all! You always have to be prepared for what comes next. Even when you've got a good map, you can still get lost.

The 10 life skills described in this book prepare you to deal with a wide range of situations. With life skills up your sleeves, you can react quicker and better, making it easier to find your way.

The Helping Hands don't drive a flying car, so you're still obliged to follow life's network of roads and paths. But, there's a very good thing that the Helping Hands can do – point you in the right direction ... forward.

Life's network of roads and paths can be pretty complicated. Take the safest roads when you start using life skills. And bear in mind that there can be many different ways to go to the same place. Later, with experience, you'll be more prepared to try out some shortcuts to go further; these are life's challenges.

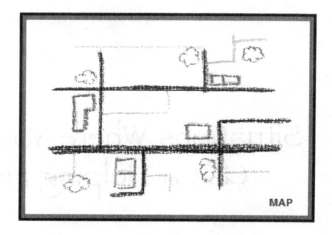

When you are learning life skills, it can be difficult to pull together your skills to react the way you want to. And there will be times when it is not clear what to do. That's why it's worth looking at examples of how life skills can be applied. Let's take some typical situations to see which life skills could help most.

What if ... you get lost?

It can be very upsetting to get lost, so how about expressing emotions for a start. If you were completely lost, your thoughts and feelings could easily go out of control, like on the emotional roller coaster. So the first thing to do is calm down.

What next? If you are lost you need to make a quick decision – what am I going to do? Take a quick look through the decision-making house. What are your options? What are the advantages and disadvantages of each option?

You will probably need to ask for help. It's time for communication. You are upset, but you still need to respect basic rules of communication. Anyone for conversational tennis?

What to do if I'm lost? =

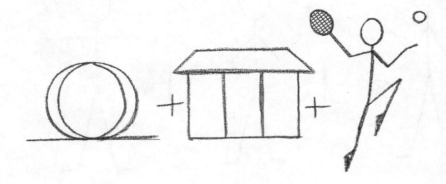

What if ... you don't have any friends?

If you find that you don't have any friends, think about caring. How well do you give and take in relationships? Remember, if you want to play a team game, at times you need to pass the ball to other team members.

To make friends, it helps to think about self-awareness. What are your likes, strengths, values...? Ask yourself the self-aware questions. Becoming more self-aware will help you to identify potential friends, people who are similar to you.

Making friends is also about empathy. You need to be able to see the I in others. Ask the self-aware questions about other people.

Making friends =

What if ... you are being bullied?

If other people are constantly trying to humiliate or hurt you, then you need to reduce stress. Remember that stressful roller coaster? Well, you're on one and it's time to get off before you start feeling ill.

If you are being bullied, you need to do some problem solving. What is causing the problem and what actions could you take to stop it happening again?

When someone calls you names or pushes you around, you have to stand up for yourself. What about communication? Have you tried to confront the bully? If you don't feel safe, ask for help from someone who is in a position to intervene on your behalf.

Dealing with a bully =

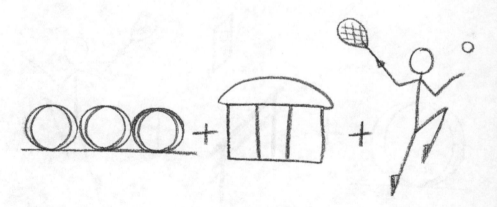

What if ... you get into an argument?

If you have a disagreement with someone, you might become angry and end up in the loop of an emotional roller coaster. Think about expressing emotions – recognise and accept your feelings, take control and calm down.

Then what? It's time to see clearly. Why are you arguing? Use some critical thinking. Think about what the other person is saying, can you see the strengths and limits of the other person's point of view?

Think about communication. Are you getting the pitch right? Are all your balls going right out of the conversational tennis court? Listen to what the other person has to say, look at them and state your point, politely, of course.

Getting out of an argument =

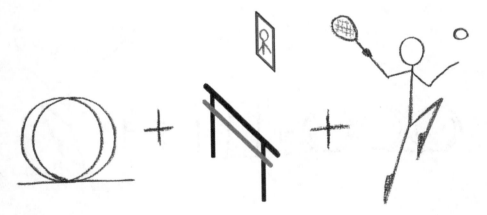

What if ... you are under pressure to work hard?

Working hard, study and tests, it's all very demanding. Sounds like it's time for reducing stress. Recognise when you feel stressed and try different ways to relax, so that you can get off that stressful roller coaster.

Think about self-awareness. Remember one of **U**'s shoes is about goals. What are your goals for the future? Think about how doing your best now will help you to achieve what you want out of life. But remember **U**'s smile – what do you like? Reward yourself with something that you like when you make progress in your work.

If the work you are being asked to do seems boring, perhaps you need to think of a way to make it more fun. What about some creative thinking? Could a new idea help you to organise your work differently?

Coping with hard work =

What if ... you have the impression that cigarettes and designer clothes make you look cool?

Some people make it look cool to wear expensive clothes, smoke cigarettes or drink alcohol. Use critical thinking to see beyond the social and emotional barriers that help to create this illusion.

If you think that someone looks really cool or uncool, think again about empathy. You need to be able to see beyond appearance and behaviour, to see a person. Someone who has made a lot of effort to show a cool image may, in fact, be shy or lacking confidence. Use empathy to see a person beneath the image.

When you are thinking about self-image, remember self-awareness. Think about your likes, strengths and values. How can you show these things as your new image?

Dealing with peer pressure =

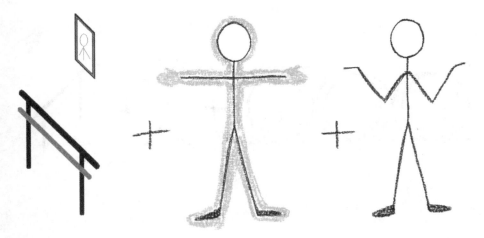

What if ... someone you know has a problem?

When someone you know is in trouble, you need to think about caring. What can you give? What can you take? Remember, the balance of give and take changes when you want to help someone. For a while, you may need to give more than you get.

To understand another person's problem, think about empathy. Can you imagine yourself with that problem? How would you feel? What could other people do to help you in this situation?

What is the best thing to do? It's time for some problem solving. What are the advantages and disadvantages of the different actions you could take to help?

Helping someone in need =

What if ... you don't know what you want from life?

If you are fed up and can't see the point in doing what other people seem to want you to do, take a step back and think about self-awareness. Who are you? What do you like to do? What are your strengths, goals and values?

Sometimes, making a few small decisions can help to unblock a situation where you are stuck in a boring routine. Have a good look through the decision-making house. What are your options for making life more interesting?

Sometimes, when you think that you've run out of ideas, a really interesting one is just waiting to be discovered in your imagination. So why not try some creative thinking, it just takes a bit of effort to clear those barriers... Can you think of a new activity that you might enjoy?

What to do with my life? =

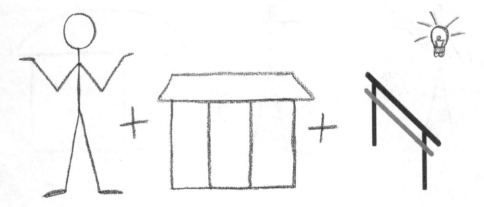

What if ... you have trouble talking with your family?

If you find that you no longer relate well to your family, think again about caring. What are you giving to help build relationships with your family? What are they giving you in return?

You need to think about communication. Are you using the basic rules of communication? Do you listen to what others have to say? Are you able to express your opinions?

When you have trouble relating to your family, you could use some problem solving. You will need to think for a bit about what has caused this problem. What could you do to get on better with your family?

How to get on better with my family =

What if ... (it's up to you now!)

Can you think of other situations where life skills come in handy?

For each situation, applying three life skills seem to be good enough to tackle the immediate needs. Combine three skills and see how much mileage it gives you for different situations.

Sometimes, you may want to use more than three skills, that's fine, just remember your aim is to deal with situations as they arise and keep moving on, so keep it simple!

There are only 10 skills on the Helping Hands, so there will be many situations that draw on the same combination of three skills. That's good for you: that is how you get plenty of use of 10 essential life skills, and become more confident.

As a reminder of such general skills, the Helping Hands can have far-reaching implications in your life. The skills are a process you go through, a kind of step-by-step guide, with no specific content tying them to one particular situation. You, the people you interact with, and the situations you experience bring all the content that determines how you apply life skills.

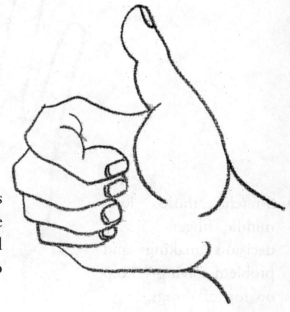

Life Skills At Your Fingertips!

If you have studied this book very thoroughly, which of course you have (haven't you?), it's time to think about what you have learned. So in a self-aware and confident style, ask yourself: What have I learned?

It's as easy as 1,2,3...

1. Your fingers can remind you about 10 life skills.

- Put your thumbs up ... for creative thinking and critical thinking – it's OK to think for yourself.

- Point your index fingers ... for communication and caring – make your point in conversation and in relationships.

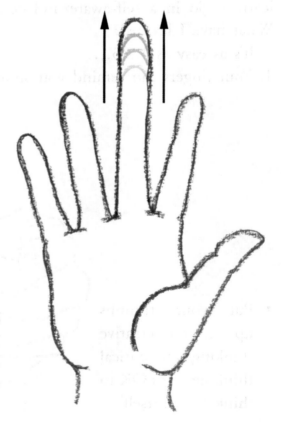

- Stretch those long middle fingers ... for decision making and problem solving – keep on top of things.

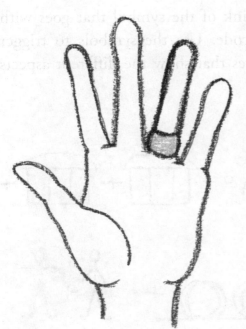

• Imagine the ringed fingers ... for expressing emotions and reducing stress – keep connected with your emotions and how you react to stress.

• Make your little fingers say I ... for self-awareness and empathy – the I in you and others.

2. Wiggle each finger and think of the symbol that goes with each skill – the life skill code. Use the symbols to trigger your memory of the pictures that show the different aspects of each life skill.

= *10 must-have life skills*

3. Like fingers, life skills work together on any task. Notice how you and others use life skills in different situations. When you are in a new or difficult situation, which three skills could help you most?

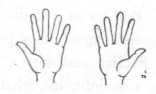

Practice Makes ... Prepared

The Helping Hands are a useful way to keep in mind 10 life skills. Learning all about these skills is a lot of work, but, it must be said, this is just the beginning. You are setting out on a learning process that's going to be useful every day of your life, for the rest of your life.

Give yourself time to learn more about life skills by using them day to day in easy situations, where you can learn from your mistakes. That way, when a difficult situation occurs, you'll be ready to apply life skills to help yourself.

The 10 pictures and accompanying symbols used in this book are a way to remember basic aspects of the must-have life skills. With a little stretch of the imagination, you can think of this as adding a layer to the Helping Hands, like a pair of gloves.

If picturing the Helping Hands is like putting on a pair of gloves, then this book offers 'one size fits all'. This can be a good way to get started. But with time, as you gain life experience, you might start noticing holes in the one-size gloves. You may just replace them by refreshing your memory of this approach, but one day you might want a pair that fits you better.

As you practice life skills, you will discover which strategies work best for you. Observe how other people use life skills – you will see what is effective and what is not. If the one-size-fits-all approach seems too tight, use what you have learned to come up with your own made-to-measure life skill code.

Does it all seem a bit serious? Well, such is life! Don't forget, life skills, like gloves, protect you from life's winters and murky waters and unknown stuff.

Do you know the saying 'practice makes perfect'? Well, as you use life skills, you'll gain confidence and you'll do better, but you'll not become perfect. Life is not perfect. The Helping Hands need to be supple enough to deal with unexpected situations.

Good luck!

Be flexible, your aim is to adapt as best as possible to your needs and the needs of others, to be ready for the ever changing demands and challenges of life. Instead of seeking perfection, you should aim to be prepared.

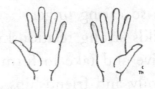

The Helping Hands Poem

Now that you know all about the Helping Hands, you shouldn't find it too difficult to learn this poem. It might help if you wiggle (or imagine wiggling) the skilled fingers as you say it.

Helping Hands

Creative-thinking thumb
Jumps barriers for me
I go beyond my peers
And let new ideas be

Critical-thinking thumb
Pushes over my past
I see merits and flaws
To clear the fog that lasts

Communicator finger
Listens and speaks with eyes
I understand the point
From hello to goodbye

Oh so caring finger
Builds strong relationships
I give and take to form
Family and friendships

Long deciding finger
Might spur me to move on
Looking at my options
I weigh up pros and cons

Problem-solving finger
Wonders which way to go
I choose the most and best
But time will do the rest

Emotional finger
Shakes with fear and delight
I allow the feeling
Then bid it a goodnight

Stress-detector finger
Goes around and around
Until I say wise thoughts
And slowly I calm down

The little I finger
Accepts me as I am
My limits and my likes
My values and dislikes

Kind empathy finger
Yells "I exist" for you
I respect your feelings
I can accept you too

These ten skilful fingers
Work and learn together
I sometimes make mistakes
That's good for goodness sake

When I am in trouble
I think about each hand
Are three fingers moving
To meet the next demand?

With able Helping Hands
I'm ready to react
Day upon day I act
To shape and share my life

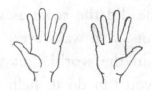

Put Your Hands Together For A Better Life

The Helping Hands are for you, to guide you day by day. But you can use them in another way… Put your hands together and think about some of the things that could be done to make life better. What would you like to see change or improve in the world around you?

The hands, being so strong and mobile, played a very important part in human evolution. They made it possible for early humans to make tools and have a big impact on their environment. Use of the hands contributed to the development of our clever human brains.

Well, the Helping Hands are very useful too. By developing the skills on the Helping Hands, you can become strong and adaptable. Use them to shape your life and, who knows, perhaps you will evolve a bit more. Like early humans, who used their hands to transform the world around them, you can make a difference.

Think about the 10 life skills described in this book; imagine all the things that you can do to help yourself and others with those skills. And, of course, if you keep on applying them in nice, healthy ways, that could mean a lot of positive things over time. Now, if everyone did the same as you to make positive contributions in lots of small ways every day, that would add up to a lot of good in the world. Put your Helping Hands together to see what you can do to help this world grow into a better place.